Firefighters!

Firefighters!

by NANCY K. ROBINSON

SCHOLASTIC BOOK SERVICES
NEW YORK · TORONTO · LONDON · AUCKLAND · SYDNEY · TOKYO

This book is fondly dedicated to the laddermen, hose teams, and cooks of Ladder 26 and Engine 58 who share a firehouse in Harlem, New York City.

ISBN: 0-590-05736-7
Copyright © 1979 by Nancy K. Robinson. All rights reserved. Published by Scholastic Book Services, a division of Scholastic Magazines, Inc.

12 11 10 9 8 7 6 5 4 3

Printed in the U.S.A.

1 2 3 4/8
07

Contents

Introduction

A fire can start almost anyplace. It can start on land, on sea, or in the sky.

There are many kinds of firefighters.

There are many jobs that firefighters do.

Firefighters shoot water from heavy hoses to knock down and control fires. They climb tall ladders and crawl through thick smoke. They cut their way through roofs and walls and into the burning cabins of ships and planes.

Firefighters jump from airplanes and dive under waterfront piers. They drive engines, ladder trucks, fireboats, and bulldozers. They race onto airport runways and busy highways. They fly helicopters and special planes called *air tankers*.

At the scene of a fire, a firefighter asks a lot of questions. He asks,

"What is burning?"

"Where will the fire travel next?"

But, the first and most important question he asks is,

"Is any life in danger?"

"Is anybody trapped by this fire?"

A firefighter's first job is to save lives.

Small Town Firefighters

It is five o'clock in the afternoon. The telephone rings in the firehouse of a small town. There is only one person in the firehouse. His job is to answer the phone.

He hears a woman's voice crying, "My house is on fire. My little boy is trapped!"

He finds out where the fire is and sends out an alarm by radio.

Around the corner, the owner of a small hardware store hears the fire report on his fire radio. He is a volunteer firefighter. He runs to the firehouse. Other firefighters arrive quickly—some from their jobs and some from their homes.

No one is paid to fight fires in this town. All the firefighters are volunteers.

The firefighters put on their work pants, rubber boots, and heavy firefighter's coats. They put on their helmets. They strap tanks filled with compressed air onto their backs. These tanks are connected to face masks. The firefighters have to breathe through these masks if the smoke is thick.

One firefighter helps another with his air tank.

9

Some firefighters climb onto the fire engine. Others climb onto the ladder truck. The engine rolls out of the firehouse. The ladder follows.

When the firefighters reach the house, they see heavy smoke coming from the first floor window. A woman is at the door.

"I can't get up the stairs," she screams. "My little boy is up there."

The stairs are blocked by fire. The fire officer finds out quickly that the fire started in the kitchen. Then it spread to the hallway and staircase.

Three things have to be done at once:
— The little boy has to be found and rescued.
— The hose crews have to get water on the fire.
— A roofman has to cut a hole in the roof.

The owner of the hardware store brings a ladder to the side of the house. His job is to find the little boy and get him out.

He forces open the window with a special tool. He climbs into the little boy's room. It is smoky. It is hard to see. He crawls on the floor and feels around. A firefighter knows

Firefighters force open windows and chop the edge of the roof to let out the heat, smoke, and gases trapped inside.

that children often hide from fire. This is the most dangerous thing they can do. The first place the firefighter searches is under the bed. He guessed right. The little boy is there — curled up and whimpering.

Gently the firefighter pulls the little boy out and carries him to the window. He places him across his chest and climbs down the ladder to safety.

The roofman has climbed another ladder and is chopping a hole in the roof with his axe. He does this to let the heat and gas escape. Otherwise the fire will spread.

11

Meanwhile, the hose crews are waiting at the bottom of the stairs with their hoses ready. As soon as the roofman has finished cutting a hole in the roof, the nozzleman pulls back a lever on the heavy brass nozzle. The water comes out in a powerful fog spray. A second hose crew takes a line into the kitchen.

Every firefighter, except the roofman, wears a mask and breathes the air from the tank on his back. He has only enough air to last twenty minutes.

But the fire is out in ten minutes.

The mother is hugging her little boy. Her dinner is ruined. The kitchen is a mess. The

Volunteer firefighters race against each other to see who can get dressed first.

house is full of water and smoke. But everyone is safe.

Volunteers spend a lot of time together. They have meetings where they elect their chief and fire officers. They have dinners and parties to raise money to buy new equipment for their firehouse.

Volunteer firefighters have to be trained to do different jobs at different fires. They study together. They compete with other volunteer fire departments in sports and firefighting contests. This is how they learn teamwork.

This is how they learn to work together to save lives.

These firefighters are called lineworkers.
Their job is to clear away anything that might burn.

Firefighters of the Wildlands

As soon as a fire is spotted in the forest or grasslands, a radio call goes out to alert firefighters: "FIRE FLASH!"

The first firefighters to attack the fire may come on foot or in a truck. These are the lineworkers. They work in teams of 25 men and women. Their job is to stop the fire.

Lineworkers use shovels, axes, and a tool called a *pulaski* which is part hoe and part axe. They use these tools to clear away anything that might burn — trees, brush, grass, and weeds. Even bare ground can catch fire, so lineworkers must dig until they reach a layer of earth called the mineral soil.

They are clearing a path around the fire. This path is called a firebreak. A fire cannot cross this firebreak because it has nothing more to burn. And when a fire has nothing to burn, it will stop.

15

Lineworkers try to keep the wind behind them so that they will not be trapped by the fire.

Lineworkers always keep an eye on the wind. They watch for sudden changes so that they will not be trapped by the fire. They know that strong winds will make their work very hard.

That is why the best time to fight a wildlands fire is at night when the wind dies down and the ground cools off. Lineworkers wear headlamps to see at night, but they use their headlamps during the day too. The thick black smoke of a forest fire can make the day as dark as night.

If a spark from the main fire starts a small

spot fire, a lineworker shovels dirt on it to smother the fire.

Other firefighters help make the firebreak. Saw crews cut down trees with power saws. Bulldozers and tractors often help to clear out a firebreak. A firebreak might have to be 100 feet wide to stop a big fire.

Sometimes the fastest way to stop a fire is to set fire to the trees and grass between the firebreak and the fire. This is called *backfiring*. A backfire starts slowly, but soon

The firing boss throws a flare to light a backfire.

rushes back to meet the main fire. With nothing left to burn, both fires will burn themselves out.

Work on the firebreak is hot and noisy. The fire roars. There is constant danger from falling trees and flying sparks.

Lineworkers wear hard hats, goggles, and headlamps. They wear heavy lace-up boots and fireshirts made of a material that will not catch fire easily. Over the shirts are brightly colored vests of yellow or orange that can be seen easily.

Lineworkers carry hand pumps, canteens of water, and small knapsacks on their backs.

Many women now work as firefighters for the United States Forest Service.

A firefighter gets into
her fire shelter.

If a firefighter is trapped by flames, he takes a small metal foil tent out of his knapsack, climbs into it, and lies down flat on the ground.

He may look like a baked potato, but the metal tent will protect him from the flames and heat for a few minutes. This is often just enough time for the fire to pass over.

No firefighter should let himself be trapped. But sometimes, this cannot be helped. Many firefighters' lives have been saved by these *fire shelters*.

Note: Fire shelters are used only out-of-doors. In a house fire or any other inside fire, a person would quickly suffocate. There would not be enough air to breathe.

Wildlands Fires: Attack from the Air

If the country is rough and there are no roads, the fastest way to get to a wildlands fire is by airplane or helicopter.

A helicopter needs a clearing to land. If there is no clearing, specially trained

firefighters jump from a helicopter while it hovers a few feet from the ground. These *helijumpers* do not wear parachutes.

Firefighters who parachute out of airplanes are called *smokejumpers*. Smokejumpers wear padded jumpsuits, helmets, and wire face masks. They wear two parachutes — one on the back and one on the front. They wear two for safety, in case one doesn't work.

In the Northwest, where the trees are tall and close together, it is dangerous to send smokejumpers. Their parachutes can get caught in the tops of trees. And it is impossible to use helijumpers.

Nowadays, some firefighters get to forest fires by climbing down long ropes that hang down from helicopters high above the trees.

If there is a clearing, a helicopter can land a group called the *helitack team* who attack the fire quickly.

A firefighter who gets to a forest fire by climbing down a long rope is called a *helirapeller*.

When smokejumpers and helijumpers arrive at a fire, their job is the same as the lineworkers. They get to work quickly to cut out a firebreak.

If there are any roads at all, fire engines called *tankers* may be sent to wildlands fires. The tanker boss may have to go off the road and drive across fields to find a lake or stream where the tanker can pump water.

But it is hard to pump water uphill; it is hard to lay hoses through rough, rocky ground and thick forest. It is often easier to bomb with water from the air.

If you were to hear fire sirens at a forest fire, the sirens might be coming from an airplane or from a helicopter. The sirens mean they are about to make a *drop*.

A mixture of water and chemicals is dropped from large buckets slung under helicopters or from tanks built right into the belly of a plane.

This mixture is not used to put out a fire. It is used to cool down the area in front of a fast-moving fire. It is used to slow down the fire so that crews can get in to build a firebreak. The mixture is colored red so that everyone can see where it has been dropped.

A plane called an *air tanker* flies ahead of the fire, and drops a mixture of water and chemicals to cool off the area.

If a fire in the wildlands cannot be controlled by the first crews, it is called an *escaped fire*. It may take days or even weeks to bring the fire under control. A large fire can burn 40,000 acres — an area equal to the city of St. Louis — in 24 hours.

It may take thousands of firefighters to fight the fire, all under the command of one Fire Boss.

Now, fighting fire begins to look like a war....

SMOKEJUMPERS parachute ahead of the fire to fight spot fires.

A helicopter makes a "bucket drop" to put out a fire behind the main fire.

Firefighters use a sm pump which pumps v from a stream.

Each team of LINEWORKERS has a CREW BOSS who watches out for their safety.

Firefighters use water pumped from fire engines called "tankers" to put out small fires.

To win the battle firefighters must surround the main fire with a path the fire cannot cross. This path is

An airplane called an AIR TANKER drops a mixture of water and chemical ahead of the fire to cool off the area. Then bulldozers and lineworkers can move up to extend the firebreak.

The AIR ATTACK BOSS is in command of the attack from the air.

The FIRE BOSS is like the general of an army. He is in command of the whole operation.

The PLANS CHIEF gives the FIRE BOSS up-to-date information on the fire.

Saw crews cut down flaming trees that might throw off sparks and start new fires.

The LINE BOSS is in charge of the attack on the fire. He may ask for help from the AIR ATTACK BOSS.

A truck called a "flat-bed transport" brings in more equipment to fight the fire.

LINEWORKERS shovel dirt on small fires to put them out.

called a firebreak or fireline. At the same time all small fires behind the main fire must be put out.

City Firefighters

Every time firefighters leave the firehouse to answer an alarm, they say they are making a *run*. There are city fire companies that make 500 runs a month, or 6,000 runs a year!

There are firefighters on duty day and night at the firehouse. They eat their meals there. They take turns working at night and

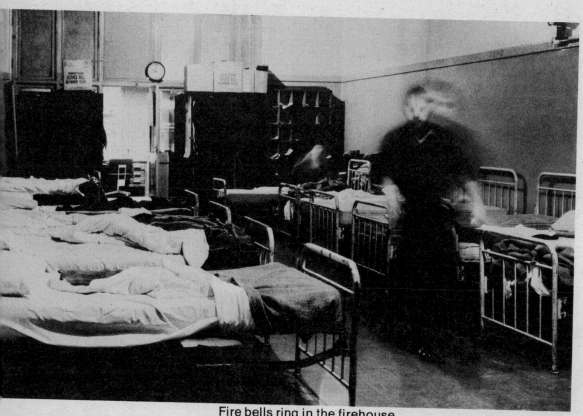

Fire bells ring in the firehouse.
Firefighters jump out of bed to answer the alarm.

In a few minutes, a ladderman is on
his way to the roof of a burning building.

sleep on cots lined up in a large room
upstairs.

An engine company and a ladder company
often share the same firehouse. But the
firefighters who ride on the fire engine do
different jobs from those who ride the ladder
truck.

27

The Engine Company

- puts water on the fire.
- keeps the fire from spreading by hosing down nearby apartments and buildings.
- covers escape paths by spraying a curtain of water between the people being rescued and the fire.

The Ladder Company

- searches the building and rescues anyone in danger.
- forces open locks, doors, and walls with special tools.
- gets rid of heat and gases from the fire by opening or knocking out windows or by cutting a hole in the roof.

The engine company has a *driver* who may also be the *pump operator*. The pump operator connects the hose lines to the hydrant. He controls the amount of water and water pressure needed to fight the fire.

The *nozzleman* is first on the hose crew. Right behind him are two or three hosemen who help him hold the hose. They are called the *back-up crew*. When a hose is filled with water, it is very heavy and hard to hold. If someone lets go of the hose, it might jump free and swing around wildly. The heavy brass nozzle could easily knock out or kill a firefighter.

The last man on a hose crew is sometimes called the *kink-chaser*. The kink-chaser makes sure the hose line doesn't get tangled or caught under a door. This could cut off the water. And, if the water is cut off suddenly, everyone is in trouble.

Good teamwork is very important to a hose crew.

A ladder company may have two firefighters driving the long aerial ladder truck — one in the front and one in the back. The driver in back is called the *tillerman.*

Roofmen have to get to the roof in a hurry. They try to get there without going inside the building. They may go up the fire escape or climb a tall ladder to the roof. If there is a building right next door, the roofmen will go through that building and cross over from one roof to the other.

This *roofman* is using his pike pole to peel off the heavy layers of tar paper on the roof.

The roofmen open roof doors and skylights to let the heat and gases escape. Often they have to cut a hole in the roof with a circular saw and use their long pike poles to push in the plaster ceiling of the top floor.

Meanwhile, other laddermen work in *search teams* to find people trapped on the fire floor or the floor above the fire. They know that smoke is the biggest killer in fires. They know that smoke travels up and through a building and gathers on the top floor. So the top floor is the next place the laddermen search. *Forcible entry teams* may have to pry open doors with Halligan tools for the search teams and the hose crews.

Most city rescues are made by leading people down the stairs or helping them off fire escapes. Sometimes portable ladders, aerial ladders, or ladders with buckets at the top are used to rescue people.

Laddermen wear flashlights on their helmets and belts around their waists. This belt is called a *life belt*. A rope can be tied onto a clamp on the belt and used in many ways. It can be attached to a tall ladder so the ladderman won't fall off, it can be tied to a doorknob in a smoky, dark room so the ladderman can find his way back, and it can be used for rescues.

Laddermen have used ropes tied to life belts to swing off a roof and rescue people waiting in windows.

Fires in Tall Buildings

During the day, thousands of people may be working in offices in a tall building. It could take more than three hours for all the people to get out of some of the tallest skyscrapers, even if they leave quietly and quickly.

A modern office building is like a chimney. Windows are often sealed shut. There are many openings and spaces between floors. Smoke can travel quickly and easily.

Practice fire drills are important in tall buildings. Each floor has a fire warden. The building has a fire safety director who makes sure the building's automatic smoke detectors and sprinkler systems are in good working condition.

The first fire officer to answer an alarm in a tall building is met at the door by the fire safety director, who tells him what is happening and shows him floor plans of the building. The fire safety director may tell people to stay where they are, if they are safe. His hardest job is to keep people calm.

Fire Chief at lobby command post talks by handi-talkie to firefighters on floors above.

An *engineman*
carries the heavy,
folded-up hose lines.

A *ladderman* lays rope on
the floor so he can find
his way back through
the dark smoky halls.

A command post is set up in the lobby. The fire officer sets up another command post, called a *staging area*, on the floor below the fire. Firefighters use handi-talkies to report to the Fire Chief at the lobby command post.

But handi-talkies don't always work in tall buildings. There is too much metal around. It can be hard to hear anything. So special hi-rise teams lay telephone lines and firefighters communicate by telephone.

At tall building fires, firefighters are worn out in 5 or 10 minutes. The heat tires them. It may be too dangerous to use the elevators. Firefighters carry heavy hoses and tools up many stories. They breathe fast and hard and use up the air in their air tanks quickly. More help is needed.

The Fire Chief radios the dispatcher at Fire Headquarters for more help. He may ask for special units such as Rescue Companies — specially trained laddermen who carry powerful tools. Often Mask Service Units bring extra air tanks and fill up the ones already used up.

The Chief will sometimes ask the dispatcher to "strike another alarm." A second, third, fourth, or fifth alarm will bring more equipment and more firefighters.

Firefighters know that even small fires in tall buildings can cause serious problems. When so many people work close together, rumors spread easily. People get scared and can do foolish things. They may hurt each other trying to get down the stairs, or block the way for the hose crews trying to get up.

Luckily, some of the worst fires in tall buildings have happened when no one was inside. A bad fire on the 21st floor of a 33-story office building in Los Angeles started at three o'clock in the morning. No one was hurt, but it took 325 firefighters from 58 companies to put it out.

A tall building may catch
fire before it is even finished!

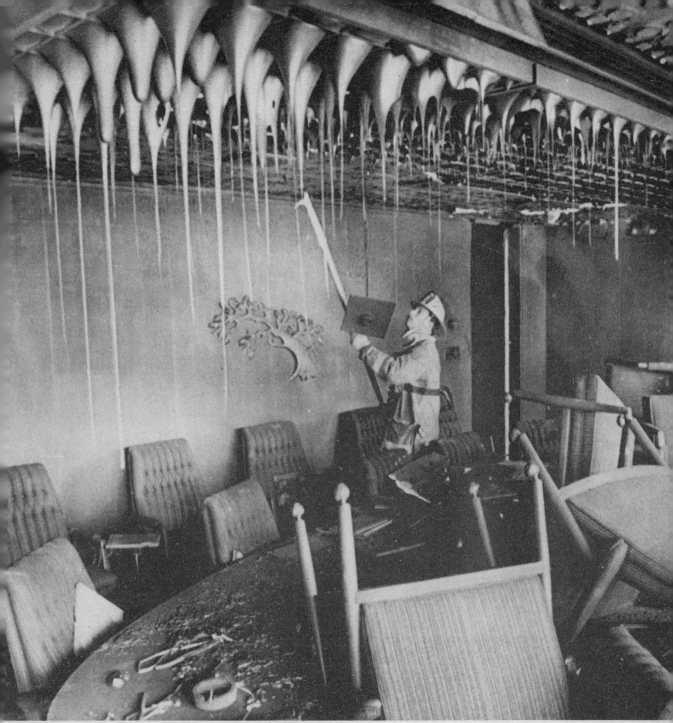

The fire in Los Angeles was so hot,
the plastic in the ceiling melted like candy.

A cargo ship runs into a tanker. This picture was
taken a few minutes after the explosion.

Firefighters on the Sea

It is a few minutes after midnight early in June. New York City firefighters are called out to fight a fire.

The flames are more than ten stories high. But it is not a fire in a tall building.

The fire is over a mile wide. But it is not a forest fire. . . .

A cargo ship has run into a tanker. Flaming oil is leaking from the tanker into the harbor. The ships are stuck together, and both ships are on fire! The mass of fire is heading for the great Verrazano Narrows Bridge.

It will take land firefighters and sea firefighters to fight this fire.

A fire engine is sent to the bridge. The firefighters hose it down to keep it cool. They help people get out of cars and off the bridge. Just in time. The burning ships pass underneath. Flames lick the underside of the bridge.

Police boats, Coast Guard tugs, and harbor tugboats all come to help.

Five fireboats answer the alarm. The first fireboat to arrive is the *Firefighter*, the most powerful piece of firefighting equipment in the world. A team of five firefighters aim her deck pipes which look like large guns. From these deck pipes this fireboat can shoot 20,000 gallons of water a minute.

The fireboat is pumping water right from the river. Three marine engineers are below deck, keeping the engines and pumps going.

The Coast Guard calls out small patrol boats to close off the channel. Coast Guard tugs and helicopters with searchlights look for people in the water.

Everyone helps. Police boats, small tugboats, and even little motorboats dash between patches of flaming oil and pull people out of the water.

The pilot of the *Firefighter* tries to get as close as he can to the burning ships. But the oil that is floating on the water is on fire, too. The deck pipes shoot streams of water at the flaming oil. The firefighters know that

A fireboat shoots water at the *Sea Witch*.

straight streams of water will not put out an oil fire. But the powerful streams can sweep the fire back and clear a path for the fireboat to get through.

For an hour, the *Firefighter* pours water on the flaming ships. Suddenly, a flashlight is seen waving on the fantail of the cargo ship, *Sea Witch*. Someone is trapped on board!

The pilot takes a chance. He noses the fireboat between the two burning ships. Everyone in the harbor watches in horror as the *Firefighter* disappears into the heavy black smoke.

The *Firefighter* pulls alongside the *Sea Witch*. Pieces of flaming cargo fall all around. The firefighters raise two ladders to the deck of the burning ship.

A man stumbles down the ladder. Another man follows him. Then another man, and another...and another.... A few minutes later, the firefighters are amazed to find they have rescued 31 sailors from the tail of the *Sea Witch*.

There were many brave acts that night. The United States government gave the *Firefighter* the Gallant Ship Award for the bravery of her crew.

It had taken hours to put out the fires that burned above deck on the *Sea Witch*. But it took weeks to put out the fires that burned way below in the cargo hold.

Firefighters couldn't pour more water onto the ship. There was already so much water, the *Sea Witch* was tipped sharply to one side. They had to pump water out or the boat would sink.

They fought the fire by cutting off the oxygen supply. Without oxygen, a fire cannot burn. Firefighters sealed off the burning compartment to keep the fire in one place and to keep more air from getting in. Then they flooded the compartment with carbon dioxide, a gas that smothers fire and will not ruin cargo.

Three weeks after the collision, the fires in the *Sea Witch* were finally out.

The powerful fireboat, FIREFIGHTER, celebrates her fortieth birthday in New York harbor.

A fire diver jumps into the water to fight a pier fire in Los Angeles.

Fire Divers

One of the hardest fires to put out is a fire on a waterfront pier where boats are unloaded. There may be crates of cargo around and oil for the ships.

Streams of water from fireboats cannot reach the underside of a pier. And this is often where the fire is burning the hottest.

The Los Angeles Fire Department was the first to use fire divers to fight pier fires.

When the fire officer of a fireboat calls, "Over the side!" a fire diver in a scuba suit jumps into the water and swims toward the pier. He pushes a float in front of him. On the float is the nozzle of a hose. The hose trails behind him and is connected to the pump of the fireboat.

As the fire diver gets close to the pier, the nozzle sends up a spray of water which acts like a curtain protecting him from the heat. He gets as close as he can and attacks the fire from below. With the help of fire divers, some pier fires have been put out in minutes instead of hours.

Some cities have fire divers whose main job is rescue. Fire divers might be called out to save someone trapped in the cabin of a sinking boat.

Fire divers never work alone. They work in pairs for safety. It is hard for them to talk

Fire divers push floats in front of them. The floats help keep the divers afloat and also keep the hose line from sinking.

with scuba masks on. But fire divers have other ways of communicating.

They write messages on white slates with black grease pencil that can be seen under water. They use hand signals. They tap on the side of a ship.

Fire divers also use rope signals. When they are searching a sunken ship, one diver enters a cabin with a rope hooked onto a loop on his back. Messages are sent back and forth by sharp tugs on the rope.

Here is a simple rope signal system used by firefighters. The word "oath" is used as a key word to help firefighters remember the signals.

One tug of the rope stands for "O" (O.K.) "Are you O.K.?" or "Yes, I'm O.K."

Two tugs of the rope stands for "A" (Advance) or "Give me more rope."

Three tugs of the rope stands for "T" (Turn back) or "I'm turning back; pull in the rope."

Four tugs of the rope stands for "H" (Help) or "Danger, get out!"

Three men walking through fire to test new space-age materials.

Firefighting in Space

A fire cannot burn in space. There is no oxygen, and fire needs oxygen to burn.

But a spacecraft carries its own oxygen. A spacecraft is full of electrical equipment and wiring that can cause fires.

When a fire on an Apollo launch pad killed three astronauts, scientists got to work to make sure this never happens again.

There had been too much pure oxygen in the *Apollo*, so they lowered the oxygen content of the air. They got rid of any materials that could burn.

Then, they tested new materials until they found fibers that would not burn easily. They covered the electrical wiring with these new materials. They used these materials in every part of the spacecraft and in the astronauts' spacesuits. Checklists were put in fireproof covers.

The scientists built full-scale models of spacecraft and set fire to them. They wanted to see how the fire would travel. They found a special paint that swells up when it gets hot. This paint can swell to 200 times its thickness. It can then block a fire and keep it from traveling through an opening or duct.

They invented automatic fire safety devices that could detect a fire and put it out before any flames showed.

The Space Shuttle is protected by Halon extinguishers. Halon is a gas that can put out almost any kind of fire with very little damage. Halon is not only used in spacecraft. It is used in computer rooms, and even in libraries.

But an astronaut cannot squirt a Halon extinguisher at a fire in the spacecraft. There is no gravity. The spray would float all around. Very little would hit the fire.

So all the equipment and wiring is in closed cabinets. In case of fire, the cabinets are automatically flooded with Halon. Some cabinets have small holes. The astronaut can fit the nozzle of a portable extinguisher into the hole and flood the cabinet.

Firefighters on Earth have been helped by the many inventions that began in the Space Program. Here are just a few:

—A new lightweight air tank and mask
—A humidity detector for forest fires that tells how dry the forest floor is
—A flying fire pump that hangs in a sling from a helicopter and can be used to fight fires on ships way out at sea.

Fire in the Sky and at the Airport

When airplanes are in the air, small fires can break out. But these fires are almost always simple fires. They are very much like fires that can happen in a home.

A passenger might drop a cigarette into the seat. Or there may be a short circuit in the electrical wiring of the food warmer.

The flight crew of the airplane has to fight the fire right away.

If a cushion is smoldering, the flight attendant may get it onto the floor quickly and pull it apart. A blanket may be used to smother the fire.

If there is an electrical fire, the attendant knows which extinguisher to use. Water and electricity can cause a shock, so the attendant grabs the carbon-dioxide extinguisher and puts the fire out in a hurry!

The real danger of a plane fire is on take-off and landing.

Airport firefighters look different from other firefighters. They wear different suits. They drive different kinds of trucks.

And they never use water on fires. They use protein foam or chemical foam.

Airport firefighters race against time. Every second counts. They must get to any point on an airfield in less than three minutes. They must get thousands of gallons of foam on the airplane right away. They must get the fire under control before they can even get close to it.

Airplane fuel — gasoline and jet fuel — is highly explosive. Even the vapors given off by these fuels can explode and burst into flames. Smoke and heat travel through a cabin quickly. People trapped inside cannot survive long.

Here are some questions people ask about airport firefighters.

During an airport practice drill, firefighters shoot water instead of foam from the turret gun of a Crash Rescue Truck.

What do airport firefighters wear?

They wear suits made of material that can stand high temperatures and direct flames. This suit, called a *bunker suit*, must cover every part of the firefighter's body.

How do they get to a fire so fast?

There is an airport firehouse no more than three minutes away from any point on the airfield. A large airport will have more than one firehouse. The whole field must be protected. Airport firefighters are never far from their trucks. When there is an alert, the doors to the firehouse open automatically. The firefighters are on the trucks getting dressed as the trucks roll out.

What are airport fire trucks like?

These trucks, called *Crash Rescue Trucks*, are built to carry thousands of gallons of protein or chemical foam. A turret gun on top can send a powerful spray of foam 200 feet. The driver can pump foam and drive at the same time.

The smaller truck, the *Quick Dash Truck*, is usually first on the airfield. It carries special rescue tools — such as a double razor for cutting seat belts and a Hurst tool. A Hurst tool looks like a set of powerful metal jaws. It can use a force of 5500 pounds of pressure to cut through metal in seconds. A Quick Dash Truck also carries chemical foam and dry power extinguishers.

What is foam?

Protein foam looks like snow and has a funny smell. It forms a blanket over the fire which smothers the fire and keeps it sealed so it will not start up again. A chemical foam called *light water* or *aqueous film-forming foam* is used more and more on gasoline fires of all kinds. Even some small volunteer fire departments carry it for automobile and truck

These airport firefighters look like science fiction monsters in their bunker suits covered with protein foam.

fires. This foam seals the fire quickly by putting a very thin layer of liquid over the fire.

Once a year every airport has a special fire drill called an *Emergency Disaster Drill*. An airplane is set on fire. Smoke bombs are set off.

Airport firefighters take part in the drill. So do local fire departments. Doctors, nurses, and emergency medical technicians are on hand. Rescue helicopters stand by. If the airport is near water, fireboats and Coast Guard tugs may be there, too.

At some airports, actors and actresses play the parts of the aircrash victims. But, at other airports, schoolchildren pretend to be the dead and injured passengers.

The airport chief tells one boy, "You have a stomach wound." A girl learns that she must pretend to have trouble breathing. The children are made up with fake blood, charcoal burns, and rubber wounds that strap on to all parts of the body. They wear torn clothing and lie all over the field. Some moan. Some lie completely still.

Now the firefighters and medical people have to go around the airfield and decide whom to help first. They have to decide how they can use their first aid supplies to save the most people. They have to decide who has to be sent to a hospital and who cannot be helped at all. Making these decisions is called *triage* (pronounced "tree-ahj").

Many airport firefighters say that the children are such good actors, they scare the life out of everyone!

"I want my mother," screams one girl at an airport Emergency Disaster Drill. Other children pretend to be dead or injured.

Firefighter Trapped

The Fire Chief arrives at a five-alarm fire. He is just in time to see a firefighter's helmet sail off the roof of an eight-story building and land in the courtyard below.

Throwing a helmet is a distress signal used by firefighters around the world.

It means, "Firefighter trapped!"

The Fire Chief asks for an immediate roll call. He learns that a captain and six firefighters are missing. It is hard for the Chief to hold back the other firefighters. They want to rush right back into the building. They want to save their friends. But the Chief knows that if they rush right back in, they will probably be in the same danger as the men who are trapped.

He must quickly plan the best way to rescue the trapped firefighters. He decides just how many firefighters to send in.

The captain and six trapped firefighters are finally dragged out. They are all unconscious. Now firefighters trained in mouth-to-mouth

A firefighter is helped to safety.

resuscitation and CPR (cardiopulmonary resuscitation) go to work. They save the lives of all seven firefighters.

All firefighters go to firefighters' training schools. They are trained in safety. They learn to keep an eye on the wind and the weather so that they will not be trapped. They learn to keep an escape route in mind at all times. They learn to handle tools carefully and wear clothing that protects them.

But there are dangers that cannot always be seen ahead of time.

There can be a sudden change in wind and weather. There may be objects, like paint cans, that explode. A floor, wall, or ceiling may collapse. Or there may be burning plastics or chemicals that give off poisonous gases.

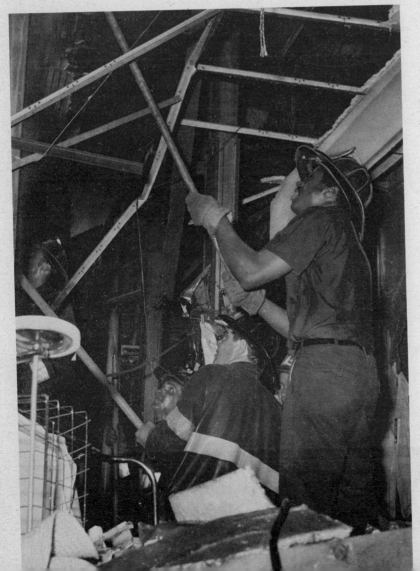

A firefighter pulls down a ceiling to check for more heat. He must make sure the fire is out.

One of the most dangerous times for all firefighters is after the main fire is out. Firefighters often have to pull down ceilings and open up walls if they think there is still some hidden heat and fire. This is called *overhaul*.

In the wildlands, checking for hot spots and breaking up embers that might burst into flames again is called *mop-up*.

During overhaul and mop-up, firefighters are tired. They can make mistakes in handling tools safely. They can slip and fall. Accidents are more likely to happen.

Firefighting is the most dangerous job there is. But most firefighters like their job. And they like each other.

In fact, firefighters are often such good friends, they feel they are part of a family and the firehouse is their home.

There is a lot of teasing in a firehouse. A visitor might be shocked at the rude nicknames firefighters often have for each other. A visitor might be surprised at the honest way they criticize each other after a fire — often in very loud voices.

When a firefighter gets back from a fire tired, wet, and dirty, it might be his turn to

These firefighters may be called
to a fire before they finish their dinner.

cook dinner for 15 ladder and enginemen!

And then, when the food is on the table, there is always someone who makes fun of it — even if it is delicious. The firefighter's feelings are hurt. He gets mad.

But a little later, the firefighter looks around the table. It is hard for him to stay mad at anyone for very long. He knows that he can count on everyone there to save his life, if he is in danger. He knows that everyone is a friend whom he needs and who needs him.

NEVER CALL THE FIRE DEPARTMENT FOR A JOKE.
WHILE THEY ARE RUSHING TO RESPOND TO YOUR
CALL, SOMEONE MAY DIE IN A REAL FIRE.

The author's deepest thanks to

Fire Department, City of New York

Forest Service, U.S. Department of Agriculture,
Washington, D.C.

Jackson Township Volunteer Fire Company #1,
Jackson Township, New Jersey

Military Sealift Command Firefighting School,
Department of the Navy, Earle, New Jersey

Nassau County Fire Service Academy

National Aeronautics and Space Administration,
Washington, D.C.

National Fire Protection Association,
Boston, Massachusetts

Port Authority of New York and New Jersey,
John F. Kennedy International Airport

Seamen's Church Institute of New York

United States Coast Guard

Woodmere Volunteer Fire Department,
Woodmere, New York

. . . and to Matt Fitzsimmons, Nancy
Osborne, and Steven Scher for their valuable help and assistance.

. . . also to James F. Casey, editor of *Fire
Engineering* magazine, John O'Hagan,
author of *Hi-Rise/Fire and Life Safety*,
and to Terry Shannon and Charles Payzant for their book, *Smokejumpers and
Fire Divers*.

. . . and to the many firefighters who
helped on this book.

Photo credits:

Cover: Jan Lukas/Rapho/Photo Researchers; 6 Syd Greenberg/Photo Researchers; 8 Everett C. Johnson; 9 Andrea Krause/Photo Researchers; 11 George E. Jones/Photo Researchers; 12, 13 Joe Licata; 14, 16-17, 19, 21 U.S. Forest Service; 18 Bob Hamber/U.S. Forest Service; bottom 17, 20, 37, 44, 54, 56, 62 UPI; 23 Lockheed-Georgia Company; 26, 27, 30 Steven Scher; 29, 36, 58, 59 Fire Department, City of New York, Fire Photo Unit; 33 Nancy K. Robinson; 34 William P. Steele; 38, 40, 41 Wide World; 43 New York Daily News; 46 Los Angeles Fire Department; 48 NASA; 52 The Port Authority of New York & New Jersey; 61 Warren Fuchs.